ANONYMIZE

YOURSELF

ANONYMIZE
YOURSELF

The Art of Anonymity to Achieve Your
Ambition in the Shadows
&
Protect Your Identity, Privacy and
Reputation

Derek Drake & Instafo

instafo

Copyright © Instafo

ISBN 978-1-094-74579-4

Printed in the United States of America

First Edition

TOP SECRET

ANONYMIZE YOURSELF

#1OperationPrecaution

<u>The 24/7 Surveillance</u>

Do you ever get the feeling that you are being watched? Well, guess what? In this era of smartphone cameras, social media, and constant electronic connectedness, *you probably are being watched!* Alright, that's probably a little bit of an overstatement, but still, it's kind of frightening when you think about it.

Just imagine how celebrities must feel. Sure, living the luxurious lifestyle of the rich and famous sounds fun. But would you believe that fame is not for everyone? There are many celebrities who wish they didn't have the constant attention that luxury and wealth bring.

Imagine having your privacy invaded every time you step out the door. Think about what it would be like to always be criticized for your beliefs, opinions, and thoughts (*if that isn't already happening to others on Facebook or Twitter!*). Famous people are under nonstop scrutiny for everything they do. Fame suddenly doesn't sound so much fun, right?

But that's a fair trade-off for fame and fortune. Or is it?

How would you feel waking up and having the paparazzi follow your every move? You can't even make certain facial expressions or have embarrassing moments without pictures showing up on social media within seconds. And then there are those pesky reporters constantly wanting your time to ask what seem like stupid questions *(thanks, TMZ!)*. Is this something you would want to deal with every day?

Unfortunately, this is the reality for actors, musicians, prominent politicians, and other famous figures.

Some people chase after fame. The cruel irony is, once they find fame, they feel <u>chased</u> by it. But if you happen to stumble upon fame, adjusting from anonymity to life in the spotlight can feel like a ride on a rickety roller coaster. *(Hold on tightly!)*

You never know when your next seemingly mundane YouTube video or Instagram pic will <u>go viral</u>. Then, suddenly, <u>you're a star</u>. Unfortunately, those very same technologies that can help you become famous can also make it easier for you to be the victim of bullies and other predators.

Now here's the conundrum: So many people want to be famous, while so many other people who already are famous wish they weren't. When it comes down to it, you may have to make the tough choice between your privacy and your career.

Therefore, whether you are grappling with the realities of fame already or wish you could transition from the spotlight back to privacy – <u>anonymity is the key</u> to being successful.

Let's take a look at why fame and celebrity aren't all they're cracked up to be, and why you should take your privacy and anonymity very seriously.

The Danger of Fame

According to Dr. Donna Rockwell, a licensed clinical psychologist, **"Fame is a dangerous drug."** (<u>https://www.psychalive.org/fame-is-a-dangerous-drug-a-phenomenological-glimpse-of-celebrity</u>) We all know that drugs can be addictive, seductive, and even consuming. Well, guess what? Fame is the same way.

Despite these dangers, our culture portrays celebrity life as glorious and glamorous. But here's the cold, hard truth:

Famous people often live shallow, empty lives. The behaviors and dangers of celebrity life can, over time, turn into actual substance abuse and addiction which, tragically, can lead to an early grave. Remember John Belushi and Chris Farley?

What's it like living the famous life?

Being famous typically means you have many friends and adoring fans, so you'll never be lonely, right? **Wrong!** In reality, being famous can be lonely and isolating, like you're living in a bubble in an ivory tower with everybody watching you, and nowhere to hide. In a way, it's ironic: everybody wants to be around you, yet you feel so isolated and alone.

<u>Face the facts:</u> Fame is downright dangerous. If you're constantly in the public eye then you are an easy target. Famous people have resources that others naturally envy and want, particularly **money**. All it takes is one bad-intention individual to feel *subjectively* offended or

slighted by you, and then, *BAM!*, you're slapped with a frivolous lawsuit.

The Media Virus

Not only do famous people have to deal with everyday people chasing after them, but they also have to deal with the **news media**.

Here's the deal: **Bad news** is more popular than **good news**. So if you do something wrong, make a mistake, or someone *lies* and says you did something wrong *(we'll get into that in just a moment)*, the media's going to be all over you like flies on a pile of *"you know what."*

Don't believe so? Then read or turn on the news, particularly the entertainment news, for a few minutes. What do you see more of, happy, positive stories or a barrage of bad news and negative headlines? It seems like the more a person appears in the news, the more endangered that person's life becomes.

Here's a news tip: Even if you aren't famous, just watching all those negative stories about famous people and even non-famous everyday Joe Schmoe (who you have never met and honestly don't care about) committing a stupid crime or being a victim of an unfortunate crime can be detrimental and depressing. Be smart and make better choices with your time than watching *useless* news that's awash with negativity solely to stimulate an emotional reaction from you that doesn't enrich your mind, like obtaining *useful* knowledge from reading books, watching informative documentaries, or learning new skills.

Now back to the lies we *referenced earlier*. False accusations are an integral part of the fame game and media ecosystem. Some scoundrel you have never met can just wake up one morning and make up some reason to sue you in court and demand money from you just because you are well-known and an easy target.

In fact, the media loves this stuff. They thrive on it. To be fair, we're not saying that all media are the **enemy of the people**, but it sure seems like more often than not, they love to shine a spotlight on the misfortunes (whether true or perceived) of the bigger whales because the higher up they are, the harder they fall – making a more sensational story.

Jealous folks are everywhere. If you have money and/or nice possessions, it shouldn't come as a surprise that other people will want a piece of what you have. And don't expect them to just ask nicely and say *please*.

The Anonymous Protection Program

The irony is if you are not famous, then you are, on the surface, a "nobody." As a seemingly "nobody," predatory people will show little to no interest in you because you *appear* to have nothing of value. It's as though being a "nobody" acts like a repellent against the evildoers.

But if you are rich and famous, you are a "somebody," so that repellent is now a pheromone attracting leechlike individuals who would love to see what they can take from you.

That's why smart and *truly wealthy* people will try to maintain a low profile and not draw attention to themselves. Likewise, not-too-smart (or *fake wealthy*) people will try to show off whatever money they have for the world to see. It's like putting a sign outside your house inviting predators to rob you.

Suddenly, being a "nobody" doesn't sound so bad after all, right? Sure, in some ways we'd all like to be "somebody" because that means you are important and perhaps powerful. But being "nobody" guards you from envious people.

Now, don't you see why it's better to maintain your privacy and anonymity rather than being in the spotlight?

Fame is dangerous. It has the capacity to destroy you. For example:

- Fame distracts you from focusing your mind on important matters that can help heal your heart, restore your soul, and help you find your pathway to internal peace.

- Fame prevents you from seeing the true value of genuine relationships as it blindfolds you from seeing how you are connected to other people in the real world.

- Fame clouds your judgment and compromises your morals, leading to safety risks, dishonest behaviors, and regretful outcomes.

- Fame becomes an addictive drug; the quest to be famous is insatiable and unsatisfactory. You will always be chasing and maintaining it to no end.

- Fame does not depict real life but instead promotes a "fake" lifestyle. You will be disconnected from everyday normal reality.

We have come to the point where you may be thinking, "Fame sounds awful. Why on earth would *anyone* want to be famous?"

<u>Here's the deal:</u> Fame itself is not inherently bad. So if you happen to find money, success, and wealth – then go for it! Just know that *fame can be very dangerous* if you don't pay attention to the risks. A disordered desire for fame and fortune is what can lead you to a downward spiral of self-destruction!

#2OperationBriefing

The Puppet-Master Approach

In the entertainment world and pop culture, you have the obviously famous musicians, actors, and other celebrities who are front and center. In Hollywood, for instance, everybody does appear to want to be seen, but there are also those higher-ups behind the scenes, working in the background and pulling the strings.

Which group would you like to belong – the celebrities in the spotlight or the folks in the background? Interesting question! Let's make this decision easier, would you take *less fame* for *more fortune*?

The truth of the matter is that there is power in anonymity, and anybody who maintains a low profile typically has the luxury to stay calm and focused. Furthermore, there is protection in invisibility, invincibility, and immunity through being anonymous.

With such assets, you can better hone yourself on creating a more productive life, plus reap these other benefits:

- **Being anonymous will allow you to experiment with new things.**

  Famous people are always under pressure to perform, entertain, and please their followers. Fame can pressure you into taking risks while everybody's watching. *Extra pressure!* When you operate out of the spotlight, that burden is lifted and you can take risks and even experiment freely without the expectations of the world riding on your shoulders.

- **Being anonymous will allow you to fail quietly and quickly.**

  Who loves to fail? Certainly, nobody does, especially when others are around. When you attempt any lofty goal without making any progress or achieving success, the ridicule from others can be discouraging and damaging and linger onward throughout the process affecting your confidence and competence. Choose to secretly fail as many times as you need to in order to get better as though nothing happens.

- **Being anonymous will allow you to enjoy your personal life.**

  You can channel all your resources and energy to learning and practicing new skills as well as doing other things you simply enjoy. Do you have a secret double life, a weird hobby, a guilty pleasure, etc.? Then that's nobody else's judgmental business but your own. This is a breather moment reminding you that you can relax and make time for yourself.

After all, isn't that what life is all about? Living it to the fullest as you deem desirable rather than under others' influence?

The Atomic Anonymous Weapon

It should come as no surprise by now that powerful (and potentially dangerous) individuals are typically the ones scheming, planning, and executing quietly while rarely being seen.

Yes, living in anonymity doesn't sound like a very exciting life. But really, living an anonymous lifestyle and operating behind the curtain is much safer than being open in the spotlight with other people out to get you.

But do you think anonymity has been an effective tool in the history of mankind?

Well, from early history to contemporary history and more recent times, anonymity has been playing this role very effectively.

Now, let's dig a little deeper into atomic anonymity and look at how it has been used as an effective weapon throughout history.

The Early-Modern History - Ancient Agents

Ancient warriors and secret spies devoted to the art of warfare, sabotage, espionage, as well as assassination have been employed throughout the ages.

One of the most famous was none other than the **Japanese shinobi,** who were devotees to their lethal art popularly known as *ninjutsu* which is translated to mean "the silent way."

This resourceful group of assassins, who we like to call "ninjas," was the true master of concealment and disguise and equipped with an arsenal of weapons and tools to engage in combat, to gain entry, to slow down the enemy, and to cause a distraction. In fact, they were the go-to mercenaries of Japan operating under the radar and clothed in mystery and confusion.

Back then, in order to delve into the secretive and anonymous world of the shinobi, one would have had to dedicate their time and life immersing in and learning about the shinobi's way, expertise, tactics, and orders. These skills were developed in secret but displayed openly when the need arose.

Multi-skilled, unsuspected, deadly, and armed with many years of training, the shinobi were a force to be reckoned with, and if you were a lord in feudal Japan and required an important task to be taken care of with finesse and stealth, the only option was the ninja, the one and only choice.

The Mid-Modern History - Secret Society

Now it's time to get acquainted with the enigmatic
Illuminati.

The Illuminati is a secretive group of individuals believed to
be seeking a totalitarian world government, referred to as
the "New World Order." The group has its membership
spanning from politicians, businessmen, to religious leaders
and other famous people. Some say the Illuminati have
infiltrated the entertainment industry and even try to use
media to brainwash the public.

The Illuminati can be traced back to Bavaria when they
were founded on May 1, 1776, by Adam Weishaupt. Even
way back then the group was believed to have been
conducting itself from the underground or background.

A government crackdown on secret societies supposedly
stifled the Illuminati in the late 1870s. Yet, many people

think that attempt to shut them down simply pushed the group more deeply into secrecy and even made them stronger.

There are critics who will tell you that the modern-day Illuminati and all its power are just a big conspiracy theory. But with so much of the organization shrouded in secrecy, who knows?

The Contemporary History - Criminal Organizations

Most of the major organized crimes successfully committed in history were planned and executed anonymously. These crimes were carefully crafted and carried out by mafias and other criminal organizations.

So, who are the biggest criminal enterprises around the globe? What strategy did they employ to be successful? What contributed to their growth and how do they make their money?

The top crime syndicates that have prospered in contemporary times include:

- Solntsevskaya Bratva of Russia
- Yamaguchi-gumi of Japan (often known as "Yakuza" in Japanese)
- Camorra of Italy
- Ndrangheta of Italy
- Sinaloa Cartel of Mexico

Anonymity is their secret weapon. If you're doing nefarious deeds, you certainly aren't going to go around and expose to the world how you operate.

Even in works of fiction like *The Godfather*, *Eastern Promises*, *Casino*, *Scarface*, and many other romanticized Hollywood films, they all have one thing in common – they guard their operations with tight secrecy.

Now as far as money is concerned, it's not easy to determine the exact amount criminal gangs make, obviously due to their meticulous nature of preventing and covering up any trail. To this day, organized criminal activities still rake over millions and even billions in revenue.

Today, with the advancement of modern technology and cryptocurrency, conducting shady businesses under the radar is easier than ever worldwide. Software such as **Tor** (www.torproject.org) can help people hide their electronic communications. If someone is buying, selling, or otherwise trading illegal activities, they definitely want to keep those transactions hidden.

> <u>Note:</u> We are not suggesting that Tor or other privacy services are responsible for criminal activity. The point is, no matter what your intentions are, there are ways to maintain your anonymity.

Having said that, there *are* bad actors out there.

Silk Road was an online "dark web" platform known as a marketplace for dealing illegal drugs. It's no longer in business, and its creator, Ross Ulbricht, will be spending the rest of his life in prison. But Silk Road wasn't the only one. Many other online black marketplaces popped up in its place.

The criminal world has evolved and is still evolving. Cyberspace makes it a lot easier for criminal organizations to work from anywhere in the world, and hidden networks provide that added security needed to establish illegal businesses anonymously.

However, organized crime shouldn't influence how you view cyber-driven evolution as there will always be pros and cons to the use of technology and tools.

The On-Going Government Agencies - Covert Operations

Do you trust the government? Most everyone has an opinion on that subject. Regardless of their trustworthiness, government agencies do engage in various tactics to keep their operations secret. Let's look at a few:

– The Central Intelligence Agency (CIA)

The CIA operates so stealthily that many people don't even know what they do. These guys are the experts at intelligence gathering around the world.

The CIA was created by the <u>National Security Act of 1947</u> to handle foreign policy intelligence and analysis, and its work includes performing covert actions. Through tactical and clever means, the CIA can subvert, sabotage, and eliminate enemies without the public knowing any specific details. *Sounds mysterious, doesn't it?*

Many of the U.S. espionage and top secret operations have focused on numerous international threats, such as the KGB, contemporary drug lords, and terrorist organizations.

– The U.S. Military and Warfare

Major events in the U.S. and international history have involved secret military missions directed by the government. These actions have led to many discoveries, the disclosure of numerous conspiracies, and even the downfall of other governments. And such operations are almost always done out of the public eye.

Not all of these secret operations have been successful. For example, there was the **Bay of Pigs Invasion** in Cuba in 1961. The attempted invasion was handled by the paramilitary group "**Brigade 2506**," which was trained and funded by the U.S. government through the CIA. Unfortunately, the effort was thwarted by the Cuban military under the command of Prime Minister (and later, President) Fidel Castro, who continued leading the island nation until finally stepping aside due to failing health in 2008.

There was **Project MKUltra,** also known as the "**CIA mind control program,**" which was a U.S. covert research operation examining the behavioral engineering of mind control in humans. Led by the CIA's Scientific Intelligence Division, Project MKUltra involved the use and administration of drugs, sexual abuse, isolation, chemicals as well as other forms of torture to test its subjects. *Scary stuff!*

All in all, government agencies' activities that are implemented to achieve certain aims will always be highly classified. So don't expect the general public to ever really know what goes on behind the scenes, nor do they need to.

The Modern-Day Example - Activist Activities

The "**Anonymous**" hacker group is an organization of people who work together for various purposes. So who are these folks? Well, Anonymous is an amorphous group of tech-savvy individuals who work together towards a common cause called "**hacktivism**" (combining "hacker" and "activism"), thus members of the group are called **"hacktivists."** A hacktivist is a person who uses tech expertise to protest against perceived societal, political, or legal injustices, censorship, and other things.

Like the name Anonymous implies, members hide their identities at all times, or at least they try to. But along the way, some members' identities have been revealed. The group has taken down many social media accounts and websites linked to ISIS and hacked major credit card companies such as Visa for refusing donations for **WikiLeaks** (an organization that publishes secret documents).

Anonymous also attacked Canada's spy agency and made public a government document which revealed confidential information about the **Canadian Security Intelligence Service.**

Anonymous has become quite well known through the secret services it provides while trying to maintain its own anonymity. Most of the members of Anonymous are faceless, nameless, and difficult to identify without a serious, in-depth investigation by law enforcement.

Example of anonymous activism is not exclusive only to the Anonymous Group; there are plenty of everyday activists and writers who take up pseudonyms in order to keep their identities shrouded in mystery while fighting for their beliefs and causes.

Anonymity and pseudo-anonymity are the *weapons to go against the tide* and the *shields to protect against outward attacks*.

The Infamous Takeaway

What do the history and background of these secret groups mean for you? They drive home the pivotal point which we have been trying to make on the effectiveness of being anonymous.

Whatever grandiose endeavor you undertake in life, try to do it without drawing too much attention to yourself *(at first, anyway)*. Execute your projects in secret. Enjoy the ease and do not worry about the blame or the failure being placed on you, until you have accomplished what you've set out to do. After all, action speaks louder than words. *Isn't it always better to be the underdog who surprises everybody in the end?*

Otherwise, if you're tempted by the urge to constantly brag about your "work in progress," you will undoubtedly attract those who will secretly work against you just to see you fail because their life is not as great as yours. Therefore, they'll want to keep you at their level or lower in order to make themselves feel better about their miserable life.

That is not to say you must become a secluded hermit and never talk to your loved ones about what you do. Share bits and pieces, but don't go overboard trying to impress, gain approval, or for other selfish-boasting reasons.

Just because you reveal something impressive about yourself doesn't mean the other person will be impressed. Oftentimes, it can have the opposite effect and can come off as an "indirect comparison insult," especially if dealing with *one* at the bottle of the totem pole.

ANONYMIZE YOURSELF

ANONYMIZE YOURSELF

#3 Operation Avoidance

There are areas in your life you ought to keep private and out of the public eye. The reason is simple: You can lead a more peaceful and successful life. Here are a few major areas that require complete anonymity.

<u>The Anonymity in Politics</u>

Is there anything more divisive than politics? It's difficult not to hear about it. Just turn on the TV news or scroll through social media and you'll see political issues all over the place.

The best thing to do is keep your political beliefs to yourself regardless of where you fall on the political spectrum. Avoiding political discussions will keep you out of the crosshairs, so to speak.

If you do choose to speak up about your political leanings, it won't take long for people who disagree with you to bear their claws. Political disagreements sometimes come down to where you are socioeconomically. If your beliefs don't benefit someone else or vice versa, then you will be at odds.

Of course, it would be silly to suggest that everybody should just agree. Political preferences will never benefit an entire population. After all, each one of us is unique, and we are entitled to our own opinions.

Even though people get can emotionally overreactive to politics without thinking, we are not suggesting you should not get involved in the political system or at least have an interest in it. Just remember that you can be in politics without trying to force everyone else to agree with you.

The Anonymity in Negativity

Have you ever been around one of those annoying folks who seem to whine and complain all day long? Well, guess what? You need to make sure that *you aren't one of them.*

Real talk. Nobody wants to be around a big whiny-pants! If you have earned the reputation as a negative Nancy, then your opinions will never benefit anyone, and others will secretly perceive you as a sore loser.

Albert Einstein once said, *"Insanity is doing the same thing over and over again and expecting different results."*

Think about it. If you're always talking negatively about other people and sharing depressing posts on social media about how terrible your life is (or bad news from the media), you are basically ruining everyone else's day by spreading bad energy and crushing their positivity.

On the surface, people may try to comfort you with words of encouragement and empathy to make you feel better. But if this negative behavior of yours is never-ending, it will eventually get tiresome and may come off as manipulative attention-seeking. You can then whine all you want about how the world needs more good-hearted and compassionate people to listen and care about your negative complaining, but even compassionate people have their limits. Simply put, the world does not revolve around you. Everybody has their own personal problems and pressing matters to deal with – such as bills to pay and family to take care of – rather than wasting their precious attention, time, and energy being gravitated towards your orbiting negative energy.

The honest truth others will never admit to you is that you are continuously making bad life decisions that are keeping you down where you are in life. So, they will be inclined to choose the <u>opposite</u> of whatever opinions you express, say, do, and agree with...simply to AVOID being led down your same path and being kept there.

Is this starting to make sense? The loudest and whiniest people on earth always seem to be the unhappiest with nothing else better to do with their time. And the people who don't spend all their time complaining always seem so much happier or at least busy being a productive member of society.

Complaining can only expose you and your weaknesses for the world to see. We all have our bad days, but instead of releasing that negative emotion like a plague out onto the world, channeling it can be the best motivation you need to focus on improving your life and achieving your success.

The Anonymity in Wealth

There's a wise old saying that *money cannot buy happiness.* That's very true. Along those lines, money also cannot buy you fame. Some of the richest people in the world intentionally keep themselves out of the public eye even though they are worth billions of dollars.

For all those well-known affluent tycoons, there are many more out there who you probably don't know, for example, Hong Kong business magnate Li Ka-shing, heiress and richest woman in Germany Susanne Klatten, American software developer John Sall, corporate-financier Carl Icahn, Swedish philanthropist Birgit Rausing, and many more. These men and women have the kind of money we can only dream of, and yet you have probably never heard of them or know how they made their fortune.

With that said, sometimes the richest people who try to stay out of the spotlight cannot remain anonymous forever. For instance, Susanne Klatten gained attention because of a complaint by German chemical company Altana's shareholders. They claimed that she had received preferential treatment when the company sold its pharmaceutical business. In the end, a Frankfurt-based court dismissed the claim. But the damage had been done. Once you're pushed into the spotlight, it's hard to slip back into anonymity.

It's important to protect everything of value that you own: money, property, and other assets. Staying out of the public eye is the security measure needed to secure your wealth.

But sometimes our ego can get in the way. There's some gratification involved when you show off your fortune. But know this or learn it the hard way: It's <u>not</u> worth it! Everyone will want a piece of it, regardless of whether they are your friends, family, or total strangers. They will even go to great lengths to get their hands on it.

They may suggest that you give them money to be charitable. And then if you refuse, they'll try to portray you as being cold-hearted and not caring about others. This "labeling" is a common manipulation tactic to try to coerce you into their demands. It all comes down to *what you have* versus *what someone else doesn't have.*

<u>**Here's the bottom line:**</u> If you do have money and valuables, don't go flaunting them for the world to see.

#4OperatonOnline

The State of Incognito

These days, it seems like *everything* is available online. Maintaining anonymity and privacy may seem impossible, but there are still some important things you can do to protect yourself in the virtual world.

You wouldn't want some of the things you say online to be connected to your offline identity because there could be serious political or economic repercussions, resulting in harassment, job loss, or even worse, threats of harm to you or your family.

Think about these scenarios:

- Addicts try to recover from their addictions in support groups.

- Human right activists try to work against suppressive governments.

- Victims of domestic violence try to escape so abusers cannot track them.

- Civil society organizations try to work to defend the course of the less privileged.

- Witnesses in protection programs try to repair their lives after experiencing crimes.

- Parents try to create a bright future for their children by any means necessary.

All of these things can be better achieved if you do them anonymously. Anonymity is critical and has the potential to save lives and minimize harm.

So it's no surprise that in the case of **McIntyre v. Ohio Elections Commission** in 1995, the Supreme Court of the United States said:

> *"Anonymity is a shield from the tyranny of the majority…*
> *It thus exemplifies the purpose behind the Bill of Rights and*
> *of the First Amendment in particular: to protect unpopular*
> *individuals from retaliation… at the hand of an intolerant*
> *society."*

Now, it is obvious that there are many offenders out there looking for innocent but famous individuals to prey on. What can you do to protect yourself?

<u>The Security Measure - Identity Theft</u>

This concept has become too common these days. Bad eggs in society will steal your personal information, pretend they are you, and then commit all types of crimes, including fraud, drug trafficking, theft, money laundering, and more. These crooks are always on the lookout to hijack your personal data such as your social security number, driver's license number, phone numbers, and credit card details.

This means that if you don't protect your personal information, you are asking for trouble. But there are ways you can protect yourself:

- **Monitor your credit card statements closely.** Some people actually pay their monthly credit card bills without reviewing all the individual charges. That's nuts! Take a critical look at every charge on your statements. If there's something on there you don't recognize, it's a clear warning sign of potential fraud.

- **Check your credit report regularly.** According to the U.S. Federal Trade Commission, you are entitled to one free copy of your credit report every 12 months from each of the three nationwide credit reporting companies. Order yours online from www.annualcreditreport.com, the only authorized website for free credit reports. By checking your credit report, you can see if someone has tried to open up a credit card account or get a loan in your name without you knowing it.

- **Update your computers regularly.** Ensure you install the latest antivirus software on your computers to detect threats. Regular updates can help both Microsoft and Apple users identify vulnerabilities. All you have to do is to visit www.support.microsoft.com or www.support.apple.com to make sure you have the latest versions.

- **Dispose of your old electronics safely.** When it's time to get a new computer or smartphone, don't just toss the old one into the trash or hand it over to a charity. You need to make sure the devices are wiped clean of all your personal information before getting rid of them. Find an electronics recycling center to wipe your data as part of the disposal process. You can search www.e-stewards.org for a certified electronics recycling drop-off center.

- **Look at email domain names carefully.** Do you ever get one of those emails claiming to be from a company you do business with, such as your bank or credit card company? You open up the email, and it has the company's logo and asks you to log in to verify certain information. *Don't do it!* It could be a fake email from a hacker trying to steal your account information. You can protect yourself by taking a closer look at the message. Look at the domain name in the "**FROM:**" field to see if it's really from the company. For example, if it's an email from PayPal then the domain should be "@paypal.com", such as support@paypal.com.

However, if it's from something suspicious, like "security@paypalsecurityalert.com" or "support@paypal.35securityupdate.com" then watch out, *it's a fake!* Remember that just because it has the words "**PayPal**" mixed into the domain, that doesn't mean it's real. Anybody can register a domain like "35securityupdate.com" then add the word "**PayPal**" as the sender (paypal@35securitypudate.com) or as a sub-domain (sender@paypal.35securityupdate.com). Hackers will try to fool you. *Don't fall for this!* Always look at the <u>ending domain name</u> followed by the ".**com**" to assess whether the email is real.

The Security Measure - Self-Destructive Social Media

It's easy to get your feelings hurt on social media. In fact, it seems like people are meaner and whinier on social media than in real life. You should be very careful about what you share online. Even seemingly harmless social media posts may give clues to culprits on how to steal your identity or track you down. Social media has killed many careers and it seems to be self-destructive.

That's not to say that social media is all bad and you shouldn't use it. On the contrary, social media sites like Facebook, Twitter, Instagram, LinkedIn, and others can be a great way to keep in contact with friends and family around the world. *But be very careful!* Sure, it's nice when people wish you happy birthday on Facebook. But do you really want identity thieves to know the month, day and year of your birth or where your children go to school?

Follow these guidelines on how to protect yourself:

- **Maintain strict privacy settings.** You should set your privacy settings – especially your personal information such as birthday or current location – in any of the social media networks to be totally private or visible to your friends only (then only your friends can wish you a happy birthday, and you don't even need to disclose the year you were born). Just go into settings and edit privacy settings in any of these social media platforms. This will ensure strangers don't have access to your private information.

- **Investigate where you appear.** Activate the incognito search mode to look yourself up online to see the result. If your picture looks strange or if there is something embarrassing, remove it. And if you see any negative comments about you, log in to your account, delete them, and consider blocking the sender.

- **Use Google Alerts to monitor your online reputation.** This allows you to always be in-the-know and notified via email whenever your name pops up somewhere. All you need is a Google account and simply go to www.google.com/alerts to set up alerts with variations of your name. For example, if your name is John Peterson Smith then you may want to set up alerts for: "John Peterson Smith", "John P. Smith", "John Smith Peterson", "Peterson John Smith", etc.

Companies do this all the time to manage their feedback and rapidly respond to criticism online in order to protect their reputation. You can also monitor your business name by setting Google Alerts with variations of your business name, such as "Smith and Sons Laundromat", "Smith Sons Laundromat", "Sons and Smith Laundromat", etc. Then if there's a disgruntled customer badmouthing your business online, you'll be alerted so you can respond, if needed.

The Security Measure - Cyberstalking

Even if you are careful not to post too much information about yourself online, that doesn't stop other people from posting about you. Some people have even made a career out of harassing, manipulating, and threatening other people by posting false accusations about them online. These cyberstalkers harass their victims through text messages, email, social media, and other forms of communications. To make things even viler, the harassment is often sexual in nature.

Stick to these best practices:

- **Never share your passwords with anybody,** not even your spouse or your best friend. If you do, change it immediately and frequently.

- **Make private any online bookings or travel itineraries.** If you tell everyone on social media what time you are leaving for vacation and exactly where you are staying, you are putting yourself at risk.

- **Do not disclose any personal data about yourself online.** Remember what we said before about checking your social media privacy settings. Don't show your full name, phone number, or address to perfect strangers.

- **Turn off automatic location settings on your phone.** If you are always tagging your social media pictures with your location, you are putting yourself at risk.

The Security Measure - Grey Market

Now we shall dive a little bit into the dark side. If you are going to venture into the grey market online, you will need to take some extra precautions to stay safe because your privacy and anonymity are imperative here.

What is the **grey market**? It's the sale or distribution of products online that are legal but done without the manufacturer's authorization.

This is where it gets tricky. *Grey market* items are "real." But *black market* items are "fake." Black market sellers will sell phony products that look like real brand names but are actually cheap knockoffs. That fancy Rolex watch on your wrist may not be so fancy after all. Grey market products are the real thing but are just being sold by unauthorized resellers.

Of course, if you are unsure about the legality of something, it's always a good idea to seek professional legal advice.

<u>Here's a hint:</u> The Tor Browser and a good virtual private network (VPN) are all you need to protect yourself with the highest level of anonymity you need. We'll explain more about what those are and how to ıse them *coming up a little later.*

#5 OperationOffline

The Unplugged Matrix

Imagine what life was like before the internet, social media, email, texting, or even landline phones. (Sounds a bit like *Gilligan's Island*, although somehow the professor managed to get the radio to work!)

What would it be like if you could disconnect from the online world? Many people would assume that having no online presence would mean you could avoid data snatchers, identity thieves, and other fraudsters. Unfortunately, that's not the case.

The good news is research has shown that there are ways you can hide your activities both online and offline.

The Protection Plan - False Impersonator

You don't have to be online to have your identity stolen or to have someone try to open up a bank account or secure a line of credit in your name without you knowing it. This heinous act can be committed by a false impersonator in the real world who is pretending to be a member or representative of an organization or claiming to have a relationship with someone you know (that illegitimate child you never knew you had until *after* you won the lottery).

Solution: Protect your personal information at all times and don't provide credit card information, bank account details, or other identifying data over the phone, unless you know for a certainty that the communication channel is secured. It's always safer to initiate the phone call yourself. For example, if you get a call claiming to be from your bank, your insurance company, or a certain institution, ask for a number or contact information online so YOU can call them back on your own time. If they refuse and say you must act now because it's urgent or a limited-time offer, be suspicious of a possible fly-by-night scam or they're not whom they're alleging to be. Don't ever make vital decisions on the fly.

The Protection Plan - Obsessive Predator

You know that stalkers are prevalent online, but don't forget that there are also plenty of them offline. Threats such as harassment and intimidation from stalkers can escalate in the real (physical) world. Some research has shown that most victims of stalking are women. In many cases, the victims are followed, intruded upon either at work or at home, put under surveillance, or harassed through phone calls.

The people committing these crimes are not merely strangers, either. Oftentimes, it's a former relationship or even a current partner who has become estranged. The crime of choice is often domestic violence.

<u>Solution:</u> The first step to stopping stalking whether online or offline is by minimizing the risk associated with it. Self-control and restraint on the side of the victim have proven to be the most effective means of bringing stalking to an end. If someone is trying to stalk you, don't fall for the bait and get into a confrontation. And by all means, call the police if someone is threatening you instead of trying to stop the person yourself. Document and report all stalking encounters. If the problem persists, get a restraining order to make it a crime for them to come near you, and to have further tangible evidence of their transgression.

The Protection Plan - Reputation Ruiner

It's not just the online world that continues to evolve. Even in this digital age, the offline world is progressing too. As long as you come into contact with other human beings, there is a risk to your reputation. If you have money and/or are successful, predators will target you and try to introduce bad things into your life.

Reputation is the king and it is still predominantly determined by what you do offline in everyday life. It is very difficult to change a bad reputation, and even the best reputation can be destroyed in a matter of minutes.

So, guard your reputation from jealous people who want to ruin it.

Solution: You can influence your reputation simply by knowing what you stand for and maintaining your congruent actions and words. Being honest, authentic, and real at all times is necessary. Be mindful with whom you associate and be judgmentally objective about their character. Yes, it's nice to see the best in everyone as society dictates us to, but that doesn't change the fact that there are still those out there who intend to do harm to others. Using the famous story of

"The Scorpion and Frog," even if you see the best in a scorpion, that doesn't mean it's not going to sting you as it's an ingrained part of its nature. Learn to see people for who they truly are and avoid the bad apples.

ANONYMIZE YOURSELF

ANONYMIZE YOURSELF

#6 Operation Tactics

The Technical Offense

According to the company's own statistics, an average of *1.49 billion* users were active on Facebook every single day in September 2018, and you were probably one of them. (https://newsroom.fb.com/company-info/) They were constantly exchanging information about their personal lives daily. And that doesn't even account for the number of daily users on the other social media platforms.

While it's convenient for staying in touch with people, such pervasive social media use can leave you vulnerable. Regardless of non-controversial topics, there are those who will not like what you post. Before long, they can invade your privacy through trolling, stalking, cyberbullying, or other means.

This invasion of your privacy is bad enough, but what amplifies the damage is when the offenders share their attacks on you with the rest of the social media universe. As a result, you may suffer emotional damage, including fear, mistrust, paranoia, depression, anger, and more.

The explosion in the use of social media certainly presents its challenges for everyone. But you can take some practical steps to protect yourself. In fact, you *should* take practical steps to protect yourself and safeguard your anonymity.

<u>**Here's a quick note:**</u> The following information can get a bit technical, but we'll try to keep it as simple and bare-bones as possible in case you aren't very tech savvy. You shouldn't ignore it, because it is <u>that important</u>.

Tactic #1: Proxy Server

Whenever you get on the internet, your connection has what's called an **"Internet Protocol (IP) address."** It's assigned by your internet provider, and it's basically how you are able to connect to the world. *Sounds simple, doesn't it?* But wait, there's something else you should know:

Your IP address isn't just a series of numbers. It can identify where you are in the world. Not just the country or even the city. With the right research, it's possible to even narrow down your location to your street or even specific address!

That's why you should use a **proxy server** which is like a *substitute for your IP address* to protect your identity. Example: If you are in the U.S. but use a proxy server in Jamaica, then sites you interact with will think your internet connection is in Jamaica.

There are <u>two types of proxy servers</u> that are important for you to know: **web-based** and **device-based**.

– Web-Based Proxy

A web-based proxy server is an online service that connects your computer to a proxy server directly through the internet. Then you can browse the web without your actual IP address being detected.

To use a web-based proxy server, all you have to do is to visit the site of the proxy service. One example is https://hide.me/en/proxy (or you can search for others online). From there you can type in the website address of the site you want to visit anonymously.

This particular web-based proxy server is perfect if you want to visit a few specific websites. You don't have to configure anything or input any technical settings on your device, just type your web address and you are good to go. Easy as can be!

– Device-Based Proxy

A device-based proxy is a more permanent solution. With device-based proxy servers, you can configure your complete computer system or any other electronic device to exclusively use a proxy server to constantly remain anonymous.

Using a device-based proxy is easy, but first, you need to register for a proxy service and pay a subscription fee. One example of a reliable proxy service is www.myprivateproxy.net (or just like with web-based proxies, there are other options online).

Then on your computer or device, go to your system settings and find your "**Proxy Settings**." Next, click on "**Change Proxy Settings**" and a pop-up window will come up. Locate "**Manual Proxy Setup**" and switch on the proxy server toggle. Type in the server address and

<u>port</u> you received from your proxy subscription, then save the settings and you are set to surf the web.

(The process may vary depending on your device. You can always do a web search for *"how to change my proxy settings"* to get instructions for your specific device.)

This same setting can be configured on your browsers, such as Chrome, Firefox, and others. Open the browser and go to browser settings. You will find "**Advanced Settings**", click on it to find a button to change your proxy settings. Look for "**LAN Settings**" and enter the proxy data.

<u>Tactic #2: Virtual Private Network (VPN)</u>

Generally, a **Virtual Private Network (VPN)** obscures your IP address far better than a proxy server does, and it works differently but achieves the same results. A VPN uses a public network to connect remote sites together.

Setting up a VPN on your computer or phone requires some work to get it configured, but the process is not too difficult. You can do it if you follow these instructions:

STEP 1: Sign up for a good VPN service. You can search for a VPN service on Google. Decent VPNs will offer you service for about $76 per year. Most require either a monthly or yearly subscription. As of this moment, here a couple of good VPN options:

– https://nordvpn.com
– https://expressvpn.com

STEP 2: After you purchase a subscription, the VPN provider will send you the details and credentials of your subscription along with instructions on how to set it up. However, the basic idea is the same with all VPN providers.

STEP 3: Go to your computer's search bar and type "VPN," then select set a **virtual private network**

connection. Go to your **phone security settings** and click to *add a connection.*

STEP 4: Enter the IP address, the domain name of the server, and the username given to you by your VPN provider. Add your authentication information which includes your password and the "Shared Secret" tool given to you by your VPN provider.

STEP 5: After these settings, hit the *connect button.* Then you can safely surf anonymously.

Tactic #3: Tor Browser

Earlier, we promised you more information about the **Tor Browser**. The Tor Browser provides multiple levels of protection to ensure your activities on the internet, location, and even identity are all kept secret and entirely private for your security.

Here are the steps required to set up your TOR Browser.

STEP 1: **Download and install.** Go to this website to download a browser from the official Tor provider: https://torproject.org/download/download.html. Close all the programs running on your computer and install it – it's pretty simple to do. Then follow the settings dialogue.

STEP 2: **Open the Tor Browser.** Keep in mind that it will take some time for it to establish an initial connection, so you'll need to be patient.

STEP 3: **Select your security level.** By default, the security of Tor is set to *low*, although it is still far more secure than conventional browsers. Just click on the green onion icon on the left side of the address bar and click on **privacy and security settings** to increase your security level.

STEP 4: **Access the .onion sites.** The most secure way to surf the web using Tor is by connecting to **.onion**

sites. These sites are "dark web" sites that are not accessible to regular search engines. You can use **DuckDuckGo** at https://3g2upl4pq6kufc4m.onion for your anonymous searches. Remember, if you click on that link now, it won't work unless you are using the Tor Browser.

<u>Here's a pro tip:</u> For advanced users, you can combine <u>Tactic #2</u> and <u>Tactic #3</u> using the Tor browser and a VPN to get maximum security and achieve the highest level of anonymity.

Tactic #4: Location Setting Deactivation

Location settings are used to monitor your exact location. When location settings are *enabled*, the Microsoft location service uses a combination of Global Positioning System (GPS), close wireless access points, and your IP address to determine your computer or device's location.

To turn the Windows location settings *off*, just go to settings and click privacy followed by location. Select "Change" and switch the setting *off* in the "**Location for this Device**" message.

On your mobile device, go to settings, click on privacy followed by location. Select location to turn it *off*.

Note: For mobile devices, location settings are vital for some everyday usages such as traveling and mapping destinations, but turn them off when not needed at home.

#7 Operation

Benchmarks

The Email Cloak

There are three ways to send an email to somebody without letting them know your real email address.

- **Use an alias** – This is a forwarding address and when you send mail using an alias, the recipient will only see your forwarding address while your real email address stays hidden. You can send an alias from any of the email services you use. Just go to the account settings of the mail service you are using and set it there; it's very simple.

- **Use a disposable email account** – You can do this just by creating a new email account using fake details and use it for the period of time you want. Then simply get rid of it. Or you can use http://dispostable.com to be your *temporary receiving email* if you don't like giving out your email address and so you don't have to go through all the hassles of creating new email accounts.

- **Use HTTPS in email client** – You can increase your level of security by using HTTPS instead of HTTP in your email client (Microsoft Outlook). Most web-based email providers such as Gmail already use this method: https://mail.google.com. This will add **SSL/TLS encryption** to all your web-based emails.

The Messaging Encryption

In addition to encrypting your email, you can also secure any instant messaging so you can remain anonymous.

- **Use TorChat** – This is a lightweight messaging client that is very easy to use, and it uses Tor's location-hiding features. Also, it makes use of SSL/TLS encryption technology. Do a search for it online and download it from there, then install it for superior anonymity.

- **Use Cryptocat** – This is a web-based instant messaging client that makes use of the AES-256 encryption technology which is very hard to decode. Cryptocat is quite suitable for all top-secret global meetings you can have with your coworkers or friends as it supports group chat. You can search for it online as well.

The File Sharing Discretion

Whenever you download files from the internet, the sender of those files will have access to your IP address. However, it is possible to download and transfer files while keeping your IP address and location hidden.

Again, just use a proxy server or a VPN to cloak your IP when downloading from a hosting site.

The Final Tidbits

Here are some final tidbit pointers:

- Don't use your real name if you are creating an account on a site you are not very familiar with.

- Don't sign up for or link to any unfamiliar account *using* your profile that already has your real personal information connected to it, like using your Facebook or Twitter profile.

- Don't disclose any information online which you wouldn't feel comfortable disclosing to a stranger in person.

#8OperationEvaluation

The Background Check

Now that you are armed with an array of tools and tips for keeping yourself out of the spotlight, your first assignment is to find out whether you are anonymous right now.

Do you ever *Google yourself?* Try it right now. Go to Google and enter your name, followed by the + (use the actual "+" symbol instead of the word "plus") and your phone number. For example: "**John Peterson Smith + 1-555-1234.**" Try other combinations with your name + your address or your birthday.

You can also try a Google image search with the same information. You can also search for your family members using these strategies to see if there is any information about you that is contained in their profiles.

Remember, you shouldn't be shy about conducting a search for yourself on social media networks. Wouldn't you rather know what's out there?

<u>The Cleanup Process</u>

If these searchers turn up any information you regard as private or sensitive, then it means your privacy might have been exposed. You can remedy this situation by:

- Contacting the website administrator where your private information is published and ask them to remove such details.

- Asking friends, family members, coworkers, and other acquaintances never to publish any information online or offline about your private life, including photos.

If sensitive personal information such as your social security number, credit card number, or bank account number is in the public domain, you can contact Google via this link and they will help you remove it.

https://support.google.com/websearch/troubleshooter/3111061

ANONYMIZE YOURSELF

#9OperationSuccess

The Medal of Anonymity

Congratulations! You have successfully completed all your operations and are now an honorary recipient of the *Medal of Anonymity*.

To briefly conclude all this – what have we learned and continuously stressed?

When you share your basic information such as your age, gender, location, address, marital status, and other personal data to the online world, you are unknowingly putting yourself out there to potential hackers, stalkers, cyberbullies, and other predators. The same applies for your information offline, which obviously you don't always have control over but should be more prudent of how you manage it.

The Protection and Prevention Act

Anonymity and privacy *protect* you from public harm by ensuring that no one will know who you are, what you represent, where you live, and know how to track you down. Also, when you're going after lofty ambition, it's best to keep it under the radar until after you have achieved it in order to *prevent* distraction and other impediments from others.

So, it is of the utmost importance that you strive for anonymity and privacy in your entire life.

Remember, the more private, secure, and anonymous you keep your personal life and information, the less susceptible you are to identity theft and other crimes.

If you've been lax about privacy already, it's never too late to get started. Act on it today!

www.ingramcontent.com/pod-product-compliance
Lightning Source LLC
Chambersburg PA
CBHW071008050326
40689CB00014B/3532